# AMAZING ARTS

## Adult Coloring Book

### Beautiful Arts for Fresh Mind and Anti-stress

# How does coloring help mindfulness?

Coloring has the ability to relax the fear center of your brain. It induces the same state as meditating by reducing the thoughts of a restless mind. This generates mindfulness and quietness, which allows your mind to get some rest after a long day at work.

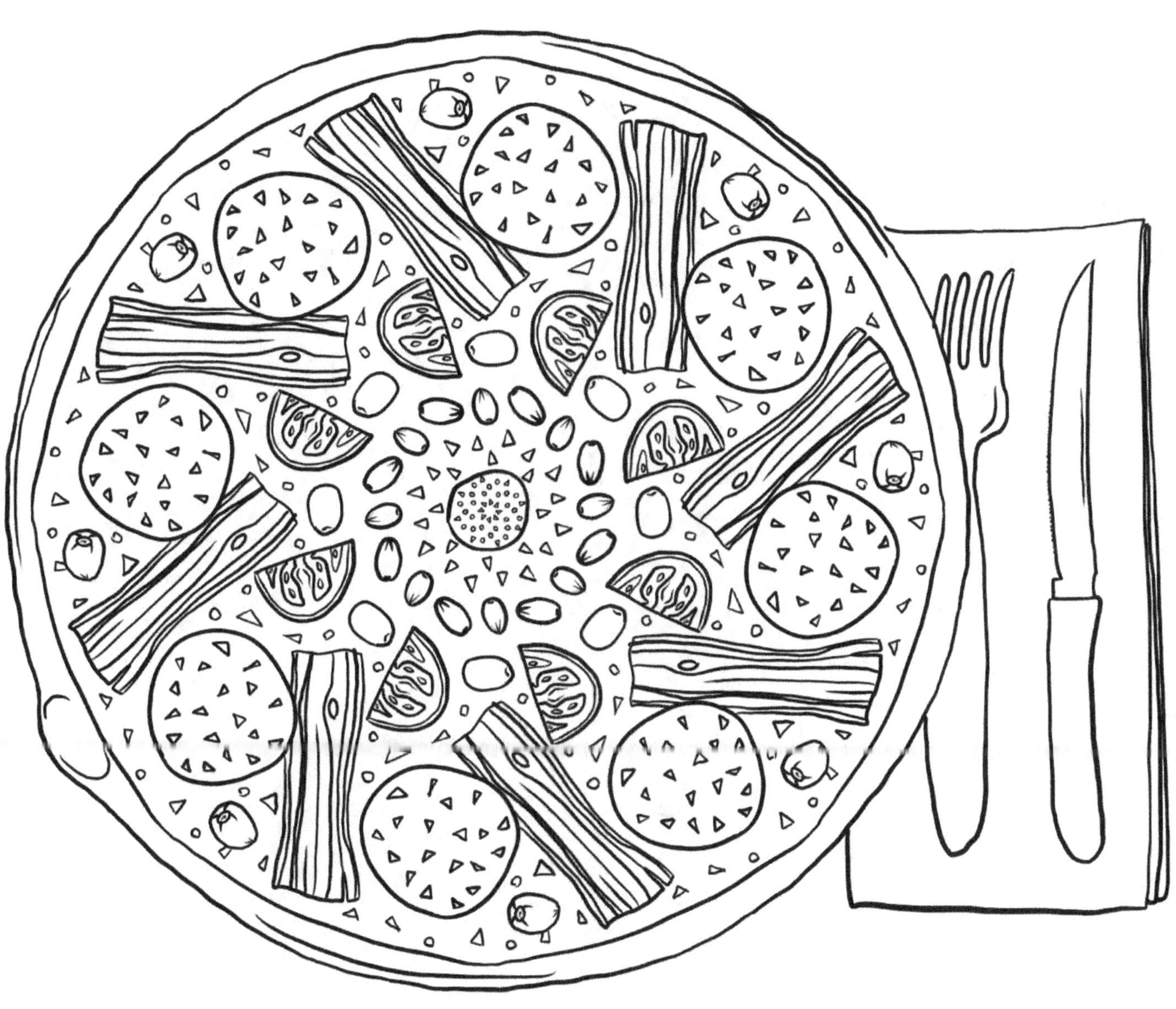